by Iain Gray

Lang**Syne**

PUBLISHING

WRITING *to* REMEMBER

Lang**Syne**

PUBLISHING

WRITING *to* REMEMBER

79 Main Street, Newtongrange,
Midlothian EH22 4NA
Tel: 0131 344 0414   Fax: 0845 075 6085
E-mail: info@lang-syne.co.uk
www.langsyneshop.co.uk

Design by Dorothy Meikle
Printed by Printwell Ltd
© Lang Syne Publishers Ltd 2016

ISBN 978-1-85217-216-9

Martin

Echoes of a far distant past
can still be found in most names

Chapter one:

Origins of Scottish surnames

by George Forbes

It all began with the Normans.

For it was they who introduced surnames into common usage more than a thousand years ago, initially based on the title of their estates, local villages and chateaux in France to distinguish and identify these landholdings, usually acquired at the point of a bloodstained sword.

Such grand descriptions also helped enhance the prestige of these arrogant warlords and generally glorify their lofty positions high above the humble serfs slaving away below in the pecking order who only had single names, often with Biblical connotations as in Pierre and Jacques.

The only descriptive distinctions among this peasantry concerned their occupations, like Pierre the swineherd or Jacques the ferryman.

The Normans themselves were originally Vikings (or Northmen) who raided, colonised and eventually settled down around the French coastline.

They had sailed up the Seine in their long-boats in 900AD under their ferocious leader Rollo and ruled the roost in north east France before sailing over to conquer England, bringing their relatively new tradition of having surnames with them.

It took another hundred years for the Normans to percolate northwards and surnames did not begin to appear in Scotland until the thirteenth century.

These adventurous knights brought an aura of chivalry with them and it was said no damsel of any distinction would marry a man unless he had at least two names.

The family names included that of Scotland's great hero Robert De Brus and his compatriots were warriors from families like the De Morevils, De Umphravils, De Berkelais, De Quincis, De Viponts and De Vaux.

As the knights settled the boundaries of

their vast estates, they took territorial names, as in Hamilton, Moray, Crawford, Cunningham, Dunbar, Ross, Wemyss, Dundas, Galloway, Renfrew, Greenhill, Hazelwood, Sandylands and Church-hill.

Other names, though not with any obvious geographical or topographical features, nevertheless derived from ancient parishes like Douglas, Forbes, Dalyell and Guthrie.

Other surnames were coined in connection with occupations, castles or legendary deeds. Stuart originated in the word steward, a prestigious post which was an integral part of any large medieval household. The same applied to Cooks, Chamberlains, Constables and Porters.

Borders towns and forts – needed in areas like the Debateable Lands which were constantly fought over by feuding local families – had their own distinctive names; and it was often from them that the resident groups took their communal titles, as in the Grahams of Annandale, the Elliots and Armstrongs of the East Marches, the Scotts and Kerrs of Teviotdale and Eskdale.

Even physical attributes crept into surnames, as in Small, Little and More (the latter
being 'beg' in Gaelic), Long or Lang, Stark, Stout,
Strong or Strang and even Jolly.

Mieklejohns would have had the strength
of several men, while Littlejohn was named
after the legendary sidekick of Robin Hood.

Colours got into the act with Black, White,
Grey, Brown and Green (Red developed into Reid,
Ruddy or Ruddiman). Blue was rare and nobody
ever wanted to be associated with yellow.

Pompous worthies took the name
Wiseman, Goodman and Goodall.

Words intimating the sons of leading fig-
ures were soon affiliated into the language as in
Johnson, Adamson, Richardson and Thomson,
while the Norman equivalent of Fitz (from the
French-Latin 'filius' meaning 'son') cropped up
in Fitzmaurice and Fitzgerald.

The prefix 'Mac' was 'son of' in
Gaelic and clans often originated with occupa-
tions – as in MacNab being sons of the Abbot,
MacPherson and MacVicar being sons of the

minister and MacIntosh being sons of the chief.

The church's influence could be found in the names Kirk, Clerk, Clarke, Bishop, Friar and Monk. Proctor came from a church official, Singer and Sangster from choristers, Gilchrist and Gillies from Christ's servant, Mitchell, Gilmory and Gilmour from servants of St Michael and Mary, Malcolm from a servant of Columba and Gillespie from a bishop's servant.

The rudimentary medical profession was represented by Barber (a trade which also once included dentistry and surgery) as well as Leech or Leitch.

Businessmen produced Merchants, Mercers, Monypennies, Chapmans, Sellers and Scales, while down at the old village watermill the names that cropped up included Miller, Walker and Fuller.

Other self explanatory trades included Coopers, Brands, Barkers, Tanners, Skinners, Brewsters and Brewers, Tailors, Saddlers, Wrights, Cartwrights, Smiths, Harpers, Joiners, Sawyers, Masons and Plumbers.

Even the scenery was utilised as in Craig, Moor, Hill, Glen, Wood and Forrest.

Rank, whether high or low, took its place with Laird, Barron, Knight, Tennant, Farmer, Husband, Granger, Grieve, Shepherd, Shearer and Fletcher.

The hunt and the chase supplied Hunter, Falconer, Fowler, Fox, Forrester, Archer and Spearman.

The renowned medieval historian Froissart, who eulogised about the romantic deeds of chivalry (and who condemned Scotland as being a poverty stricken wasteland), once sniffily dismissed the peasantry of his native France as the jacquerie (or the jacques-without-names) but it was these same humble folk who ended up over-throwing the arrogant aristocracy.

In the olden days, only the blueblooded knights of antiquity were entitled to full, proper names, both Christian and surnames, but with the passing of time and a more egalitarian, less feudal atmosphere, more respectful and worthy titles spread throughout the populace as a whole.

Echoes of a far distant past can still be found in most names and they can be borne with pride in commemoration of past generations who fought and toiled in some capacity or other to make our nation what it now is, for good or ill.

Chapter two:

For the Stuart cause

Bearers of the surname of Martin can lay claim to rather warlike origins, in the form of Mars, the mighty Roman god of war, from whom the name is derived.

The champion of military power and conquest, Mars also had a more peaceful aspect, as a protector of farmers, while his son, Romulus, is believed to have built the walls of Rome.

A common forename from early times, it increased in popularity in the early Christian era in veneration of the fourth century St. Martin of Tours and, in common with many forenames, or Christian names, was also gradually adopted as a surname.

It is recorded in Scotland as early as the twelfth century, when two Martins served in the court of William the Lyon, who reigned from 1165 until 1214, while its Gaelic form of

MacMartin ('son of Martin') was found in the Highlands and Islands.

In later centuries, many MacMartins adopted the more common Lowland form of Martin.

Another form of the name was MacGillemartin, indicating devotion to St. Martin, and one interesting study has found that the spread of this name throughout the Highlands and Islands closely followed the route of the early Christian missionaries.

It is with the MacMartins/Martins of the often lonely and inhospitable Highlands and Islands that much of the romance and drama associated with the name are to be found, through their close kinship with the two proud clans of the Camerons and the MacDonalds.

As kinsfolk of these clans, the MacMartins/Martins were destined to share in not only their glorious fortunes over the turbulent centuries of Scotland's history, but also their tragic misfortunes.

It is with Clan Cameron, whose crest is a

sheaf of five arrows and whose motto is 'Unite', that the Martin link is particularly strong, and this makes them heirs to a proud, but often bloody, tradition.

The clan had for centuries held lands in the Lochaber region, mainly around Loch Lochy, and it was a Sir John de Cameron who in 1321 was one of the signatories of that resounding clarion call of Scotland's freedom known as the Declaration of Arbroath.

Ninety years later, the Camerons and their kinsfolk such as the Martins took part in one of the most savage battles ever fought on Scottish soil, the battle of Harlaw, fought on July 24, 1411.

Also known as the Battle of Red Harlaw because of the blood spilled, no side emerged victorious.

Donald MacDonald, 2nd Lord of the Isles, had mustered about 6000 of his best clansmen and burned Inverness after crossing to the mainland and marching up the Great Glen.

His strength swelled to 10,000 after other clansmen including Camerons, Chattans,

MacIntoshes, and MacLeods joined him. Promising them rich pickings, MacDonald marched them towards Aberdeen.

The Earl of Mar hastily assembled a force that included northeast lairds while the Provost of Aberdeen also raised men.

The opposing forces met just north of Aberdeen, and battle was joined shortly after the summer sun had risen.

The fearless and ferocious clansmen repeatedly charged the ranks of the Earl of Mar and his men, only to be cut down in swathes, but not before exacting their own toll in blood.

As the sun sank low in the west, both sides were exhausted and had to retire from the fray, leaving behind a battlefield littered with the corpses of at least 1,000 clansmen and 600 of Mar's men.

The Martins also fought under the colours of Sir Ewen Cameron of Lochiel, 17th Chief of Clan Cameron, at the battle of Killiecrankie.

Following the so-called 'Glorious Revolution' of 1688 that brought William of

Orange and his wife Mary to the thrones of England and Scotland, John Graham of Claverhouse, Viscount Dundee, raised the Royal Standard in favour of the exiled Stuart monarch James VII and II.

Gathering a 2,500-strong force of clansmen that included a contingent from Clan Cameron, he engaged a 4,500-strong government force under General Hugh Mackay of Scourie at the Pass of Killiecrankie on July 27, 1689.

Brave, but undisciplined, the clansmen fired off a volley of musket fire before throwing the muskets to the ground and rushing pell-mell down hill into Mackay's closely packed ranks.

The clansmen were mown down in their hundreds by the disciplined musket fire of Mackay's troopers, but not before inflicting equally heavy losses.

Both sides suffered terribly in the battle and the outcome proved to be inconclusive, but, fatally for the cause of the exiled Stuart king, 'Bonnie Dundee' died the next day from his wounds.

Jacobite unrest in Scotland intensified following the Hanoverian succession to the throne under George, Elector of Hanover, in 1714, and in September of the following year John, the 11th Earl of Mar, raised the Standard of James VIII and III, the 'Old Pretender', at Braemar.

Mar raised an impressive force in excess of 10,000 men, including Camerons and their kinsmen such as the Martins under the leadership of John, the son of the 17th chief who had fought at Killiecrankie.

The Jacobite ranks were plagued by bad leadership and lack of a coherent strategy, however, and the cause was effectively lost following the battle of Sheriffmuir on November 13, after Mar lost the initiative by withdrawing north to Perth.

The Old Pretender landed at Peterhead in December, later travelling to Perth where he held a dispirited court for three weeks before departing for foreign shores, never to return.

It was Donald Cameron, known to posterity as 'the Gentle Lochiel', and whose father had fought for the Old Pretender, who let his heart rule his head and, against his better judgement, supported the doomed cause of the Young Pretender, Prince Charles Edward Stuart, during the abortive Jacobite Rising of 1745 to 1746.

The prince had landed on the small Outer Hebridean island of Eriskay on July 22, 1745, landing on the mainland at Loch nan Uamh three days later.

It was vital for him to receive the armed support of the powerful clan chiefs in his quest to restore the Royal House of Stuart to the throne, and one of his first visitors was the Gentle Lochiel.

Although Lochiel welcomed his prince with all due respect, he informed him that without an army at his back he should never have come.

The angry prince is said to have retorted: 'In a few days, with the few friends that I have, I will erect the royal standard and proclaim to the people of Britain that Charles Stuart is come over to claim the crown of his ancestors, to win it or perish in the attempt', adding that Lochiel could stay at home and learn the fate of his prince from the newspapers.

His Highland pride stung by this, Lochiel replied: 'No! I will share the fate of my prince and so shall every man over whom nature or fortune has given me any power!'

The Stuart Standard was raised a few weeks later, on August 19, at Glenfinnan, on Loch Shiel, and Lochiel and his 800 clansmen and kinsmen such as the MacMartins were among the first to rally to it.

They were destined to pay a bloody price for their support, however, when Jacobite hopes were dashed forever at the battle of Culloden,

Raising the Standard at Glenfinnan

fought on Drummossie Moor, near Inverness, on April 16, 1746.

In what was the last major battle fought on British soil, hundreds of clansmen died on the battlefield while hundreds of others died later from their wounds and the brutal treatment of their government captors.

The official muster roll for the Jacobite army records no less than seventeen MacMartins serving in Cameron of Lochiel's Regiment, while a number of Martins/MacMartins are recorded as having served in other Jacobite regiments.

These include four Martins with the Duke of Perth's Regiment; a David Martin from Montrose who served with the Forfarshire (Ogilvy's) Regiment; a 42-year-old John Martin from Stonehaven who served under the colours of the Ecossais Royale, that had been raised by Lord John Drummond when he landed with a force at Montrose in November of 1745, and a John Martin who served with Stoneywood's Aberdeen Regiment.

Chapter three:

Lords of the Isles

The MacMartins/Martins are also recognised as having kinship with the once mighty Clan MacDonald, more properly known as Clan Donald.

A mailed hand firmly grasping a cross is the crest and 'By sea and by land' is the motto of this clan whose nine branches include the MacDonalds of Sleat, the MacDonalds of Clanranald, the MacDonalds of Glengarry, and the MacDonalds of Keppoch, and it is to the MacDonalds of Sleat that the MacMartin/Martin link is particularly strong.

The MacDonalds and their kinsfolk of today such as the Martins can trace an exotic lineage back to Donald, grandson of Somerled, King of the Isles, who was known as the Summer Wanderer because of his extensive seafaring exploits.

The clan had assumed the title of Lords

of the Isles by the fourteenth century and, as masters of a sprawling fiefdom, ruled a confederacy of clans.

Much of their power resided in the fact that from their base at Dunyveg, on the south of the west coast island of Islay, they controlled a strategic sea route between the north of Ireland and Scotland's western seaboard.

Ruling imperiously as monarchs in their own right, it was not until 1476 that John of the Isles was forced to accept the authority of the Crown.

This incurred the wrath of his volatile and bastard son, Angus Og, who raised rebellion against both his father and James III, winning a famous victory over them in 1484 at the battle of Badh na Fala (Bloody Bay), near Tobermory, on the Sound of Mull.

Described as 'a man of singularly violent and bloodthirsty character', Angus met a particularly bloodthirsty end in 1490 when his own Irish harper slit his throat while he was asleep.

The harper, in turn, suffered the horrific punishment of being torn apart, limb from limb, by wild horses.

By 1493 the situation on the western seaboard had reached such a stage of virtual anarchy, with royal authority flouted at every turn, that an exasperated James IV finally annexed the Lordship of the Isles to the Crown, with the monarch himself assuming the title of Lord of the Isles.

The MacDonald power was broken, but it would be at least another century before peace was brought to the isles as rival clans sought to exploit the power vacuum that resulted from the break-up.

As late as 1568, James VI expressed his contempt for his wild and unruly subjects in the far-flung Highlands and Islands when he wrote: 'As for the Highlands, I shortly comprehend them all in two sorts of people.

'The one that dwelleth in our main land, that are barbarous for the most part, and yet mixed with some show of civility: the other, that dwelleth in the isles, that are utterly barbarous, without any sort of show of civility.'

Under duress, the leading chiefs such as the MacDonalds eventually found they had little option but to agree to a series of measures aimed at pacifying their disorderly lifestyle.

These measures were contained in the Statutes of Iona of 1609 and reinforced by parallel legislation of 1616.

Following a meeting on Iona with Andrew Knox, Bishop of the Isles, nine leading men including MacDonald of Dunyveg, subscribed to the statutes – drawn up to remedy 'the neglect of all duty to God and of his true worship and the growth of all kind of vice.'

Measures adopted to pacify the restless natives of the Western Isles and Highlands included the provision of inns, or hostels, for the traveller, a ban on carrying pistols unless on government service, provision for clergy to be 'paid and obeyed' and churches rebuilt.

Living at free quarters on the poor – or 'sorning' was to be treated as thieving. No chief was to be allowed to own more than one birling, or galley, of 16 or 18 oars, while they were also required to have a fixed residence.

More insidious however, were some of the other measures to be enforced. The traditional bard, keeper of a clan's glorious traditions, was to be banned and treated in the same league as beggars and other 'idlers'.

These bards were to be imprisoned, their ears cut off, and banished – facing death by hanging if they returned.

Under parallel legislation of 1616 an attempt was made through a special Education Act to further eradicate Highland culture by replacing Gaelic with English.

Translation of the Bible into Gaelic, for example, was banned.

Reasoning that much of the Highland unrest could be quelled over time by attempting to turn the youth into 'little Lowlanders' it was enacted that the eldest son or daughter of leading men should be educated in the Lowlands.

But despite the harsh measures imposed

on clan chieftains by successive Stuart monarchs, their loyalty to the dynasty proved unswerving.

In common with the Camerons and their Martin kinsfolk, the MacDonalds and their kinsfolk fought at the battle of Killiecrankie and gave their support to the abortive Jacobite Rising of 1715.

Thirty years later, MacDonald of Sleat refused to call out his clan in the 1745 Rising, but MacDonald of Clanranald, MacDonald of Glencoe, MacDonnell of Glengarry, and MacDonell of Keppoch raised Jacobite regiments.

The muster roll for the Jacobite army of 1745 to 1746 shows two MacMartins served in MacDonald of Clanranald's Regiment, while a Martin MacMartin served with MacDonell of Keppoch's Regiment.

Chapter four:

On the world stage

As the various winds of war swept over Scotland, some Martins found time for rather more creative and constructive pursuits.

Foremost among them was the rather oddly named **Martin Martin**, born at Bealach, near Duntulm, on Skye.

The exact date of his birth is not known, but it is known that he died in 1719 and that it was in 1695 that he published his famous *A Description of the Western Isles of Scotland*.

A graduate of Edinburgh University and Leyden University, Martin was a geographer and a mapmaker, and his monumental work remains an extremely valuable source of material for historical researchers.

Far from the Western Isles that Martin Martin so graphically described, generations of Martins have achieved fame in a variety of fields, particularly in the world of entertainment.

Dino Paul Crocetti, born in Steubenville, Ohio, in 1917, is better known as the late American actor and singer **Dean Martin**.

Along with Sammy Davis Jnr. and Frank Sinatra, Martin was a member of the famous Hollywood 'Rat Pack', and starred in films such as *The Young Lions*, *Rio Bravo*, and *Ocean's Eleven*.

Martin, who died in 1995, is particularly remembered as a hugely popular singer, recording more than 100 albums and 500 songs including his 'signature tune' of *Everybody Loves Somebody*.

Millicent Martin is the English actress, singer, and comedienne, born in 1934, who first rose to fame as the resident singer in the British television satire *That Was The Week That Was*, while in recent years she has appeared in American television sitcoms such as *Frasier* and *Will and Grace*.

Born in San Juan, Puerto Rico, in 1971 as Enrique Jose Martin Morales, **Ricky Martin** is the singer who has became a major star in the world of what is known as 'Latin Pop' music, while **Chris Martin**, born in Devon in 1977, is the lead singer, pianist, and rhythm guitarist with the British band Coldplay.

Married to the actress Gwyneth Paltrow, he is also a leading spokesperson on issues of fair trade.

Also in the world of music, **Sir George Martin**, born in 1926, is the English record producer sometimes referred to as 'the fifth Beatle' because of his work as producer of almost all the Beatles' records.

It was as manager of the Parlophone record label that he signed the Liverpool band up in 1962, after they had been turned down by the Decca label.

Born in 1922 at Battle Creek, Michigan, **Dick Martin** is the American comedian who co-hosted the groundbreaking comedy and variety show *Rowan and Martin's Laugh-In*, from 1968 until 1973.

Also in the world of comedy is **Steve Martin**, born at Waco, Texas, in 1945 and raised in Garden Grove, California, and who is the multi-talented writer, film producer, actor, comedian, and composer, whose many film credits include *The Jerk*, *Dead Men Don't Wear Plaid*, *Roxanne*, and, in 2005, *Shopgirl*.

He is also a contributor to the prestigious *The New Yorker* magazine.